I SPY
SUPER EXTREME
CHALLENGER!
A BOOK OF PICTURE RIDDLES

Photographs by Walter Wick

Riddles by Jean Marzollo

I Spy Super Challenger!
and
I Spy Extreme Challenger!

Cartwheel
·B·O·O·K·S·®

SCHOLASTIC INC.

New York   Toronto   London   Auckland   Sydney
Mexico City   New Delhi   Hong Kong   Buenos Aires

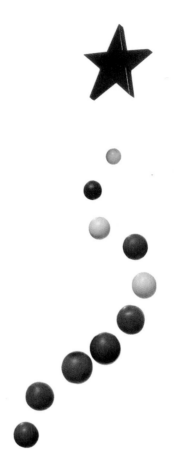

Book design by Carol Devine Carson

I Spy Super Challenger! (ISBN: 0-590-34128-6)
Text copyright © 1997 by Jean Marzollo.
"Tiny Toys," "Silhouettes," and "Toys in the Attic" from *I Spy* © 1992 by Walter Wick; "Stocking Stuffers" from *I Spy Christmas* © 1992 by Walter Wick; "Peanuts and Popcorn" from *I Spy Fun House* © 1993 by Walter Wick; "Chain Reaction," "The Hidden Clue," and "A Whale of a Tale" from *I Spy Mystery* © 1993 by Walter Wick; "Flight of Fancy" and "City Blocks" from *I Spy Fantasy* © 1994 by Walter Wick; "Storybook Theater" and "1, 2, 3" from *I Spy School Days* © 1995 by Walter Wick. All published by Scholastic Inc.

I Spy Extreme Challenger! (ISBN: 0-439-19900-X)
Text copyright © 2000 by Jean Marzollo.
"Make Believe" and "Odd and Ends" from *I Spy* © 1992 by Walter Wick; "Christmas Crafts" from *I Spy Christmas* © 1992 by Walter Wick; "Creepy, Crawly Cave" and "The Laughing Clown" from *I Spy Fun House* © 1993 by Walter Wick; "Masquerade," "The Mysterious Monster," and "The Toy Box Solution" from *I Spy Mystery* © 1993 by Walter Wick; "Monster Workshop" and "Yikes!" from *I Spy Fantasy* © 1994 by Walter Wick; "Old-Fashioned School" from *I Spy School Days* © 1995 by Walter Wick; "A Secret Cupboard" from *I Spy Spooky Night* © 1996 by Walter Wick. All published by Scholastic Inc.

Library of Congress Cataloging-in-Publication Data is available.

ISBN-13: 978-0-545-09890-8
ISBN-10: 0-545-09890-4
12 11 10 9 7 6 5 4 3 2 1   9 10 11 12 13
Printed in Singapore • This collection first printing, January 2009

TABLE OF CONTENTS

Picture riddles fill this book;
Turn the pages! Take a look!

Use your mind, use your eye;
Read the riddles—play I SPY!

For Zoë and Eva Morozko
————————
W.W.

For Ricky
and Zhao Hong
————————
J.M.

I SPY

SUPER
CHALLENGER!

I spy a hydrant, an iron, a dart,
Two cowboy boots, a little glass heart;

Three birds, a bell, a beetle, a B,
A flame, and the Roman numeral III.

I spy three dogs, two cleaners for pipes,
A baby asleep, the Stars and Stripes;

Eyes with no face, a fireman's axe,
A trotting globe, and ten little jacks.

I spy two ladders, a duck and its twin,

A mousetrap, a sailor, a tiny clothespin;

A candle, a pipe, a watchband, a ball,
And a towering clown who will soon take a fall.

I spy a limo, a mouse, and a rock,

Two bows, a boat, a bee on a block;

A pencil, a golf tee, a church with a cross,
A jingle bell, and chocolate sauce.

I spy a penguin, a fine-tooth comb,

A zipper pull tab, and a little bird's home;

A cone from a sweetshop, a cone from a tree,
A bow tie, a tiger, a mouse, and a G.

I spy an apple, a house of bricks,

Four candy canes, and eight craft sticks;

An owl, a dragon, a cricket, a bee,
Musical notes, and the number 3.

I spy two spurs, two dogs, two 8's,
Four red hands, four tops, two skates;

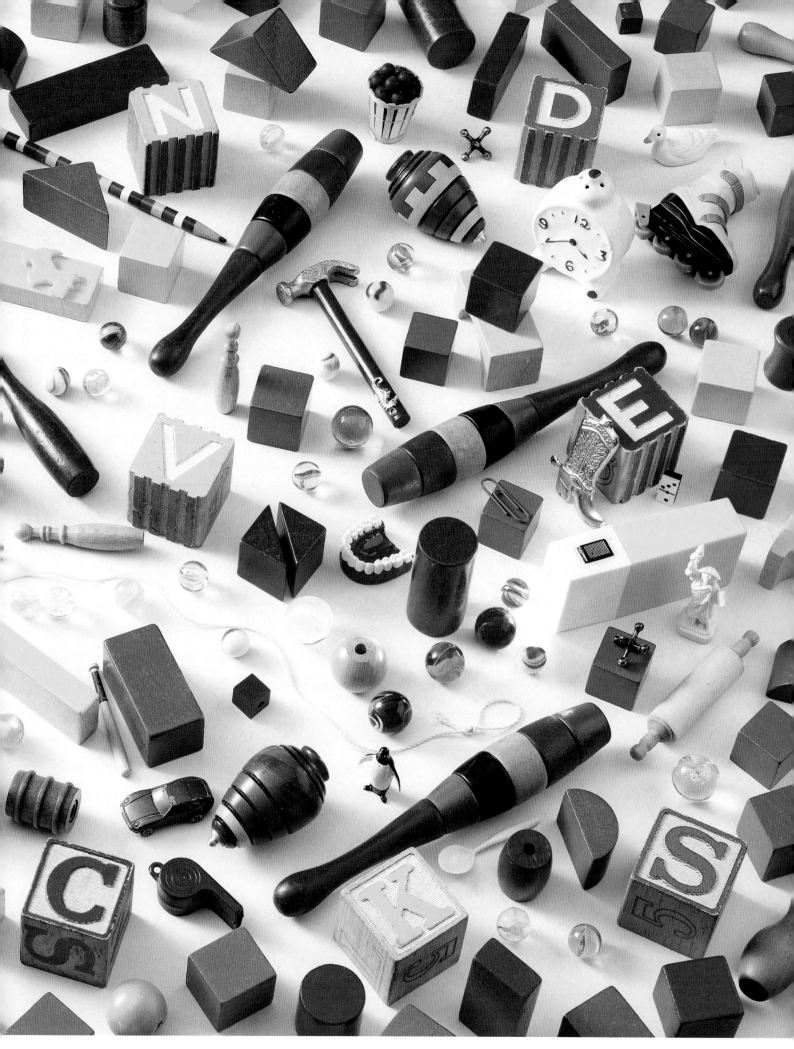

An off-on switch, a see-through trunk,
A paper clip, and a statue that shrunk.

I spy two snowmen, a walnut, a horn,

Paper-clip skates, an ear of corn;

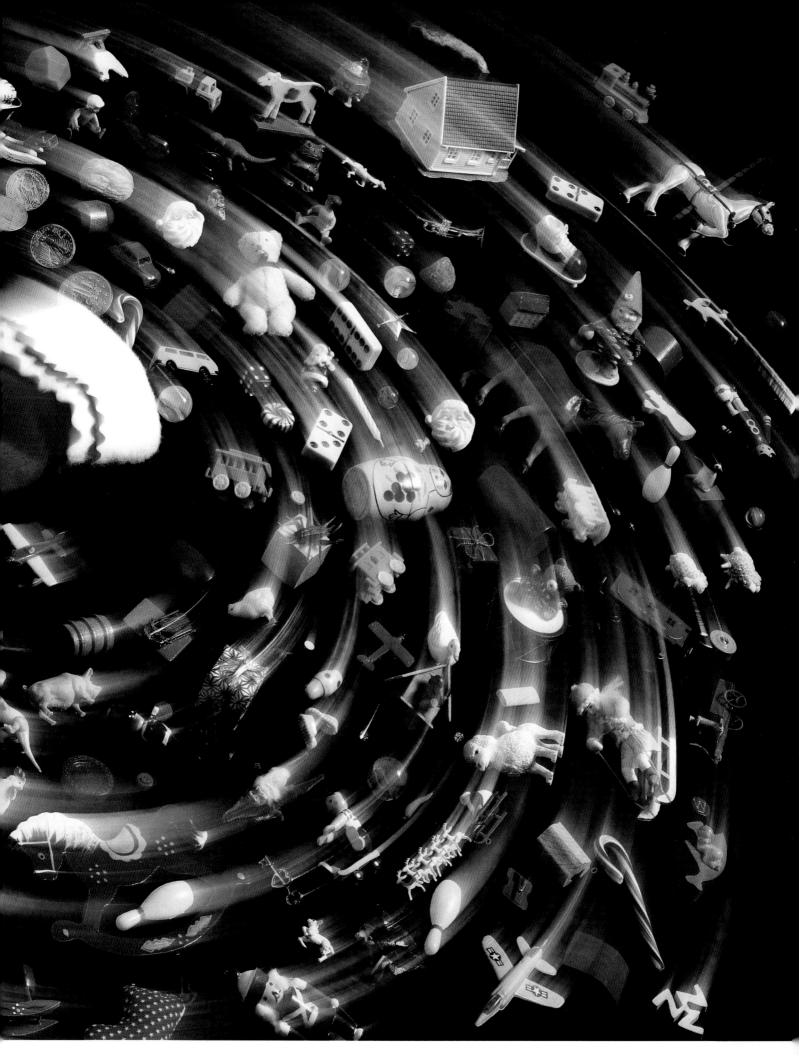

A birthday candle, a brown-and-white dog,
A cricket, a soccer ball, and a hog.

21

I spy a bat, a balloon, a pail,

A box of potatoes, a horse's tail;

Two umbrellas, a little spare tire,
A baby bottle, ICE, and Fire.

I spy a nut, thirteen number 9's,
Twenty-five spades, and three road signs;

Two pennies, two cacti, four arrows, a stork,
Six dominoes, five flags, and a fork.

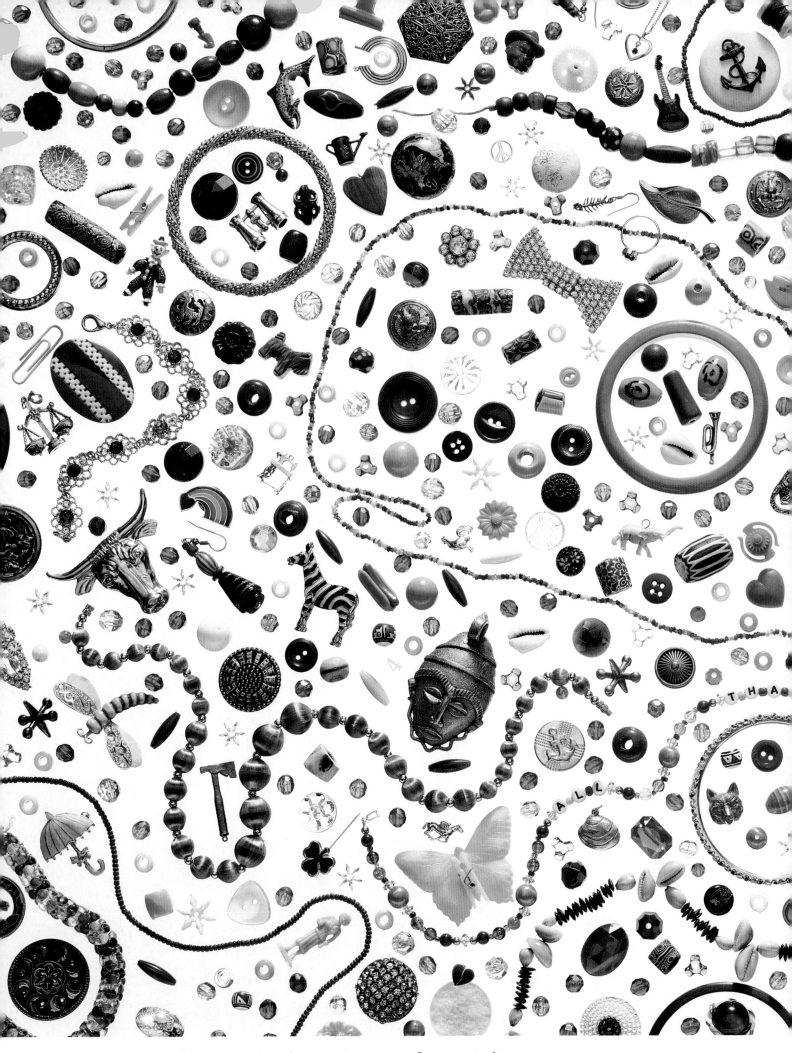

I spy three clothespins, a fast-riding man,
A wooden heart, and a watering can;

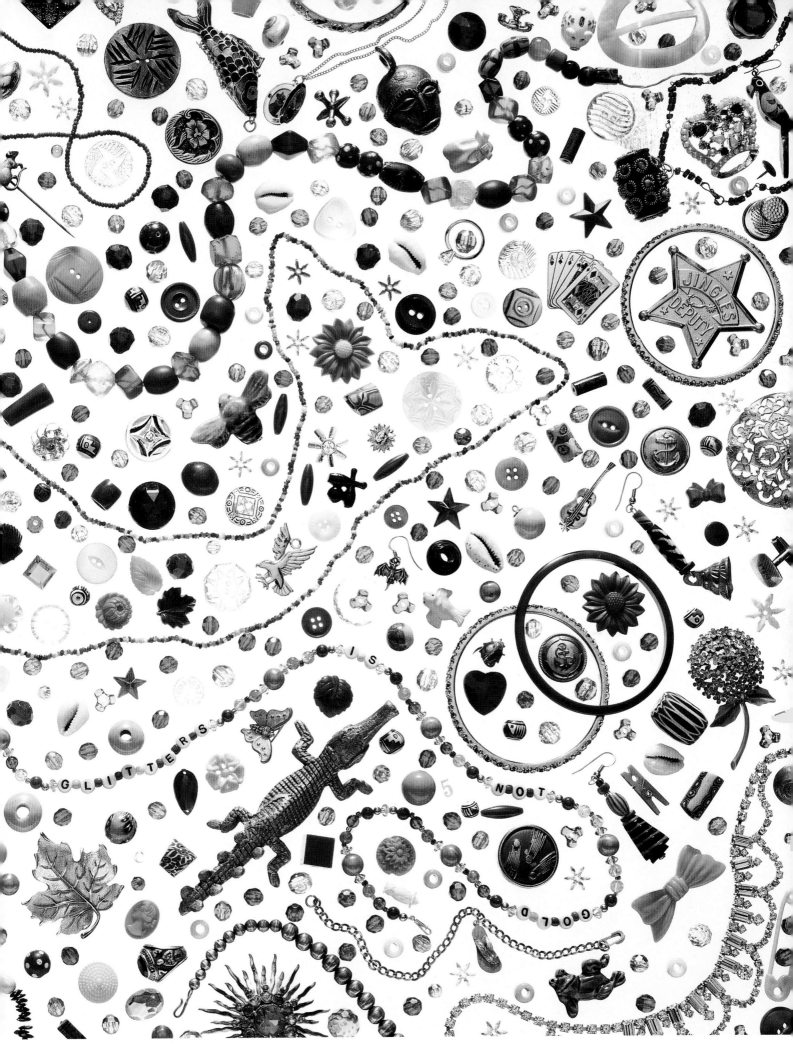

A safety pin, a shiny blue hat,
A rat, a cat, a bat, and ALL THAT.

I spy a pumpkin, a white wooden chair,

Miss LAZYBONES, and a boot in the air;

A running dish, a hammer, a plane,
And hardest of all, a PAGE with a train.

EXTRA CREDIT RIDDLES

Find the Pictures That Go With These Riddles:

I spy an acorn, a telephone toy,

A key, and an angel drummer boy.

I spy a rainbow, a bird that is blue,

Ballet slippers, and binoculars, too.

I spy a blue boot, a small fish with fins,

A jump rope, and ten white bowling pins.

I spy a sea horse, teeth, and a V,

A domino, and a wooden D.

I spy a flag and a small puzzle piece,

Three barrels, two hens, and worn-out fleece.

I spy a peeking giraffe, a truck,

Six red shoes, and a little blue duck.

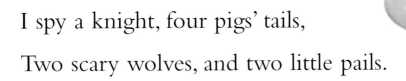

I spy a knight, four pigs' tails,

Two scary wolves, and two little pails.

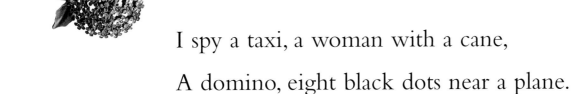

I spy a taxi, a woman with a cane,

A domino, eight black dots near a plane.

I spy a horseshoe, a broom, four B's,

OIL, eight crab legs, and three little trees.

I spy a strainer, the point of a pen,

A wrench, a zebra, and three sportsmen.

I spy three mice, a tortoise, a hare,

An itchy colt, and a climbing bear.

I spy a sandal, a game-board shoe,

A grand piano, and Pegasus, too.

To Adkins Isaac Word,
James Adkins Word

———————

W.W.

For Drayton and Sam 1999
and Elizabeth and Michael 2000

———————

J.M.

I SPY

EXTREME CHALLENGER!

I spy two clothespins, a busted clock tower,
Five jacks, a pie, Pegasus, a flower;

Two gears, two dice, two buns, a car,
A stern octagon, and the shadow of a star.

I spy a camera, a sewing machine,
A chain, a hammer, and 113;

Three lions, a ruler, a bottle of glue,
An elephant's trunk, and a buffalo, too.

I spy a saddle, a backwards B,

A Ferris wheel, and a tiger T;

A ladybug, a ticket, a goat,
Eight H's, three tees, and a photographer's coat.

I spy two pyramids, a baseball, a snail,
Three 22's, and a musical scale;

Four buttons, an arrow, and Harry's test,
A top, a whip, a compass, and BEST.

I spy a fishhook, a fingernail clipper,
A trophy, a timer, the top of a zipper;

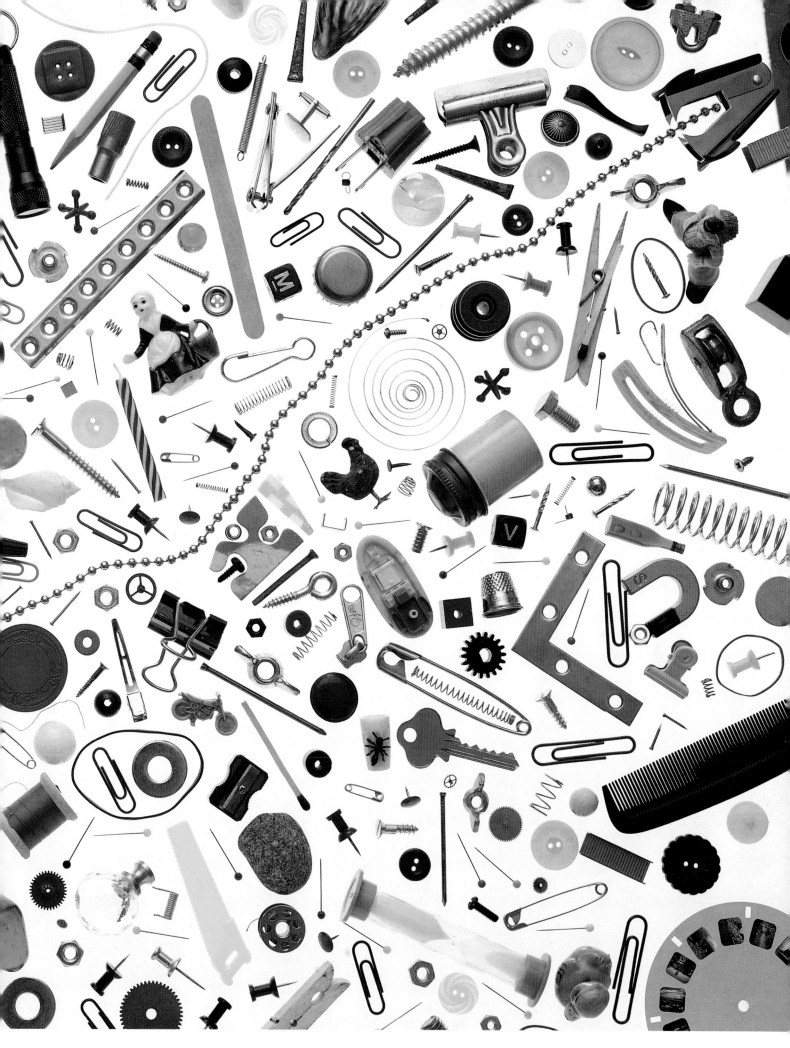

A bent straight pin, two bubbles, a bell,
Five erasers, a needle, a sword, and a shell.

I spy two thimbles, two timers, two dice,
Four birds, three tops, two jacks, six mice;

A pig, a nut, a guitar, an ace,
A wrench, and a missing bottle's space.

I spy a sharpener, a shoelace, a kitten,
Tape, a crayon, two gloves, and a mitten;

Three fancy dogs, a rocking-horse mane,
Two quilted stars, and a man in a plane.

I spy a gyroscope's shadow of blue,
A flamingo, two springs, and a kangaroo;

A hook, a toothbrush, a cat, a key,
A stegosaurus, and a sword from the sea.

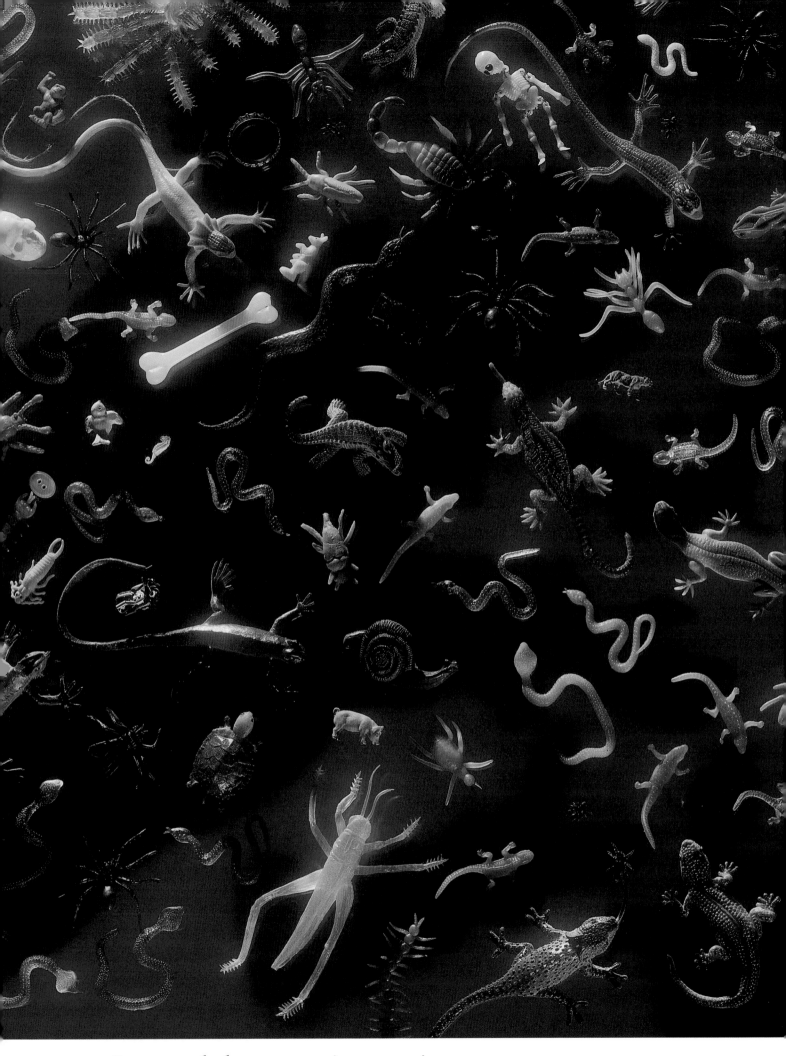

I spy a lobster, a pig, a guitar,

Two skulls, a button, a spring, a car;

Eleven spiders, a rabbit, a cat,
A woolly mammoth, and a shadowy bat.

I spy a clothespin, a button that's red,

A thimble, a nail file, a wee turtle's head;

Three pair of earrings, four bow ties,
A moustache, a frog, and two mousey eyes.

I spy a thumbtack, a pig, bear ears,
A spoon, a heart, a 3, and three gears;

Two button eyes, puffball shoes,
Two forked tongues, and sad blue ooze.

I spy a windmill, a compass, a cane,
An arrowhead, a lunchbox, a chain;

A xylophone, two keys, three bases,
Binoculars, and two starry places.

EXTRA CREDIT RIDDLES

Find the Pictures That Go With These Riddles:

I spy an airplane, a face with no hands,

A chicken, a cherry, and six rubber bands.

I spy two leaves, a black guitar,

XYLOPHONE, and a little blue star.

I spy a fan, a fish, six 4's,

A paper clip, and three dinosaurs.

I spy a football, a repeated phrase,

Two acorns, two pumpkins, and ten sunny rays.

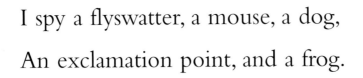

I spy a flyswatter, a mouse, a dog,

An exclamation point, and a frog.

I spy a doll, three coins that shine,

Two question marks, and a division sign.

I spy a bag, a paper-dot tail,

Two plastic bows, a pin, and a nail.

I spy a giraffe and an ape for the zoo,

A marble, two mice, and a motorcycle, too.

I spy a yellow musical note,

Fourteen marbles, a brush, and a boat.

I spy a motorcycle, a lovely pearl ring,

A single eyeball, and a brown-and-gold wing.

I spy a needle, three windows of red,

Antlers, five fans, and a little elf's head.

I spy a clothespin, a spool of thread,

LA ARAÑA, a bear, and UNCLE NED.

Write Your Own Picture Riddles

There are many more hidden objects and many more possibilities
for riddles in this book. Write some rhyming picture riddles
yourself, and try them out with friends.

The Story of I Spy Challenger Books

For years children who have found every single thing in every single *I Spy* book have
begged for a harder book to challenge their visual and mental skills. Consequently,
Walter Wick and Jean Marzollo selected from previous *I Spy* books the hardest pictures—
the ones with the most objects. Jean Marzollo then asked children in second and third
grade to tell her which objects were the most difficult to find. With their comments
and eager spirit in mind, she wrote brand-new rhyming riddles. Warning to grown-ups: If
this book is too hard for you, enlist some children to help.

Acknowledgments for *I Spy Super Challenger!*

We'd like to thank the many children and their teachers who tested these riddles for us: William, Isaac, Tommi Ann, Alessandra, Rebecca, Geoffrey, Chad, Ian, Tom, Amanda, Robbie, Jeff, Caitlin, Laila, Owen, and Mrs. Donna Norkeliunas; Kerry, Dani, Ryan, David, Sasha, Sam, Ray, Matt W., Lucas, Maike, Jo, Desi, Lana, Kim, Erica, Marty, Billy, Sophie, Rachael, Matt H., Jasen, Matt A., and Ms. Brennan; Jordan, Lee, Justine, Erin, Ryan, Adrienne, Brandon, Katie, Hannah, and Greyson. We'd also like to thank David Marzollo for his outstanding creative input.

Acknowledgments for *I Spy Extreme Challenger!*

We would like to thank the following hard-working I Spy hunters for testing the riddles in this book: Kayla Allen, Melanie Bozsik, Chris Brennan, Jody Dew, Richard Donohue, Ian Gallagher, Brendan Galvin, Max Garfinkle, Kimberly Hyatt, Stefan Jimenez, Brian Levine, Michael Lyons, Amber McCoy-Snapp, Samuel Mell, Olivia Seymour, Kaitlyn Shortell, Darius Szkolnicki, Averyann Zuvic, and their third-grade teacher, Nancy Radtke; Michelle, Jennifer, and Donna Cotennec; Chris and Molly Nowak; Phoebe Zoe Little; Claudio Marzollo; and, once again, David Marzollo for his extremely creative output.

Jean Marzollo and Walter Wick

About the Creators of *I Spy*

Jean Marzollo has written many award-winning children's books, including thirteen I Spy books, eight I Spy Little books, and eleven I Spy readers. She has also written *I Love You: A Rebus Poem*, illustrated by Suse MacDonald; *I Am Planet Earth*, illustrated by Judith Moffatt; *Happy Birthday, Martin Luther King*, illustrated by Brian Pinkney; *Thanksgiving Cats*, illustrated by Hans Wilhelm; *Shanna's Princess Show* and *Shanna's Doctor Show*, illustrated by Shane Evans; *Pretend You're a Cat*, illustrated by Jerry Pinkney; *Mama Mama*, illustrated by Laura Regan; *Home Sweet Home*, illustrated by Ashley Wolff; *Soccer Sam*, illustrated by Blanche Sims; and *Close Your Eyes*, illustrated by Susan Jeffers. Most recently she has written and illustrated a highly acclaimed series of Bible stories for young children. For nineteen years, Jean Marzollo and Carol Carson produced Scholastic's kindergarten magazine, *Let's Find Out*. Ms. Marzollo holds a masters degree from the Harvard Graduate School of Education. She is the 2000 recipient of the Rip Van Winkle Award presented by the School Library Media Specialists of Southeastern New York. She lives with her husband, Claudio, in New York State's Hudson Valley.

Walter Wick is the photographer of the I Spy Books. He is the author and photographer of *A Drop of Water: A Book of Science and Wonder*, which won the *Boston Globe/Horn Book* Award for Nonfiction, was named a Notable Children's Book by the American Library Association, and was selected as an Orbis Pictus Honor Book and a CBC/NSTA Outstanding Science Trade Book for Children. *Walter Wick's Optical Tricks*, a book of photographic illusions, was named a Best Illustrated Children's Book by the *New York Times* Book Review, was recognized as a Notable Children's Book by the American Library Association, and received many awards, including the Platinum Award from the Oppenheim Toy Portfolio, a Young Reader's Award from *Scientific American*, a *Bulletin* Blue Ribbon, and a Parent's Choice Silver Honor. His most recent series, Can You See What I See?, has appeared on the *New York Times* Bestseller List. Mr. Wick has invented photographic games for *Games* magazine and photographed covers for books and magazines, including *Newsweek*, *Discover*, and *Psychology Today*. A graduate of Paier College of Art, Mr. Wick lives with his wife, Linda, in Connecticut.

Carol Devine Carson, the book designer for the I Spy series, is art director for a major publishing house in New York City.

I Spy Books for All Ages:
I SPY: A BOOK OF PICTURE RIDDLES
I SPY CHRISTMAS
I SPY EXTREME CHALLENGER!
I SPY FANTASY
I SPY FUN HOUSE
I SPY GOLD CHALLENGER!
I SPY MYSTERY
I SPY SCHOOL DAYS
I SPY SPOOKY NIGHT
I SPY SUPER CHALLENGER!
I SPY TREASURE HUNT
I SPY ULTIMATE CHALLENGER!
I SPY YEAR-ROUND CHALLENGER!

I Spy Books for New Readers:
I SPY A BALLOON
I SPY A BUTTERFLY
I SPY A CANDY CANE
I SPY A DINOSAUR'S EYE
I SPY FUNNY TEETH
I SPY LIGHTNING IN THE SKY
I SPY MERRY CHRISTMAS
I SPY A PENGUIN
I SPY A PUMPKIN
I SPY SANTA CLAUS
I SPY A SCARY MONSTER
I SPY A SCHOOL BUS

And I Spy Books for the Youngest Child:
I SPY LITTLE ANIMALS
I SPY LITTLE BOOK
I SPY LITTLE BUNNIES
I SPY LITTLE CHRISTMAS
I SPY LITTLE HEARTS
I SPY LITTLE LEARNING BOX
I SPY LITTLE LETTERS
I SPY LITTLE NUMBERS
I SPY LITTLE WHEELS

Also available:
I SPY CHALLENGER! FOR GAME BOY® ADVANCE
I SPY JUNIOR: PUPPET PLAYHOUSE CD-ROM
I SPY JUNIOR CD-ROM
I SPY PHONICS FUN
I SPY SCHOOL DAYS CD-ROM
I SPY SPOOKY MANSION CD-ROM
I SPY TREASURE HUNT CD-ROM